# RISE AGAIN

reflections of a reclusive mind
that found release

SAEE JOSHI

Writer's Pocket

First published by Writer's Pocket in 2023

email: publish@writerspocket.com



cover design by Purva Dudhrejiya



ISBN-13: 978-93-6083-336-7



www.writerspocket.com

***This Book Is Dedicated To:***

1. My family and friends who have seen me through all my seasons, and yet, have been nothing but supportive and encouraging towards me throughout this journey.

2. My parents - My Aai and Papa,
Who taught me how to dream and encouraged me to follow my heart wherever I go.
But most importantly for being my guiding light and lifting me up during my darkest times. Thank you for all the times you believed in me, especially when I just couldn't find it in me to believe in myself.

3. My Grandfathers (Late Ramkrishna Joshi and Late Chandrashekar Verulkar) and my dearest cat sister, Magnoleah,
For recognizing my talents long before I learnt how to spell and for always encouraging me to keep writing through every circumstance in life.
(If you can read this in heaven, may my words reflect a journey that makes you proud, or so I can only hope.)

4. And finally, My Dear Readers,
Especially for those wondering if I have written about them…
If you're wondering, then I definitely have!

Hope you enjoy reading this book as much as I enjoyed writing it.

*May you sail through all the storms,*
*That are too heavy to speak about,*
*That are too deep to trench through.*
*By faith, through grace,*
*May you find love, light and solace.*

**- From one healing heart to another.**

CONTENTS

## PART I FLIGHT: The Takeoff



## PART II FLIGHT: The Crash

## PART III FLIGHT: The Rise Again

# ACKNOWLEDGMENTS

What started out as one of the most challenging experiences of my life soon turned into a rewarding journey of self-discovery. One that I still find hard to truly fathom!

I'd like to start by thanking my incredible parents. For inspiring me to be the best version of myself. I am eternally grateful to them for everything they have done for me. But most of all for being by my side at my lowest lows and highest highs, for providing their guiding light throughout my life, and believing in me, especially when I just could not believe in myself.

I would like to thank my younger brother, Sumedh for his constant support, advice and love. From helping me ease my worries and mental blocks to supporting my random and bizarre ideas at every turn of life! Thank you for being my support system and my true protector throughout my life. I love you always.

None of this would have been possible without my good friend, Shivangi, who helped familiarize me with the publishing process and has played a massive role in my personal growth these last few years. I am eternally grateful to you always. I wouldn't be writing this today without you!

Not to mention, a huge thank you to my wonderful friends who kept me going and sane throughout this process. You guys know who you are.

Thank you for being an integral part to this book getting done in one piece!

A big thank you to everyone on the Writer's Pocket team for giving me this unbelievable opportunity. A special thanks to Mahek, and Mohit, for their excellent publishing advice and management throughout. Thank you for turning this dream into reality!

I would like to extend my gratitude to my current team at digitalfarm, the current company I work in, with a special mention to my managers, Cxyza and Abeda, for their guidance and support in refining the writer within me and for playing a major role in my growth during the past year.

Finally, to all the beautiful people in my life. I would like to thank them for bearing with me and for making me the writer that I am today.

I could not have asked for better people to accompany me on this beautiful journey.

A big thank you to everyone who trusted me enough to help me rebuild the same trust in myself again.

# PART I
## FLIGHT: The Takeoff

*I've travelled the world,*
*Filling my cup with,*
*New experiences,*
*New people,*
*New places.*

*Never stopping,*
*Never pausing,*
*Not even for a second.*
*To breathe, to love,*
*to truly live,*
*For myself.*

*Carrying others pain and sorrow,*
*Solving everyone's problems,*
*Meeting the worlds expectations,*
*While abandoning my own.*

*Wishing to fly away,*
*To find myself.*
*Not realizing,*
*How I'd lost pieces of myself,*
*Throughout my flights.*

*The weight of the world suddenly,*
*Felt all too heavy,*
*I couldn't possibly keep flying,*
*With broken wings,*
*And wounds that ran too deep,*
*Made me too numb to feel.*

*Now I want to fly away*
*From this reality*
*From the world*
*From the torture*
*of surviving with broken dreams,*
*Shattered hopes,*
*And a faltered me.*

# 1. Pieces of Me

*Do you run away to far off places?*
*Lose yourself in familiar faces?*
*Get too caught up in the mess*
*That's you can't regress.*
*Carrying burdens of society*
*Pleasing people who won't carry you*
*Cause you can't find peace*
*In your own silence.*
*All my life I've tried to escape*
*Thinking I'd find myself*
*Anywhere I, anywhere I go.*

*Leaving behind,*
*Pieces of me*
*Didn't even realize*
*I'd been running away from me.*

*Through these pieces of me*
*I didn't even realize*
*I'd been running away*

*I didn't realize how much I'd lost*
*Until I was alone in the dark*
*My chest tightened*
*As I cried uncontrollably*

*All my life I've tried to escape*
*Thinking I'd find myself*
*Anywhere I, anywhere I go*

*Leaving behind,*
*Pieces of me*
*Didn't even realize*
*I'd been running*
*Away from me.*
*Through these pieces of me*
*I didn't even realize*
*I'd been running away.*

*In my darkest of hours,*
*Broken, scared and lost,*
*I'd no choice but to deep dive within*
*Gathered myself,*
*Piece by piece,*
*Faced my shadows*
*Set myself free*

*All my life I've tried to escape*
*Thinking I'd find myself*
*Anywhere I, anywhere I go*

*Leaving behind,*
*Pieces of me*
*Didn't even realize*
*I'd been running*
*Away from me.*
*Through these pieces of me*
*I didn't even realize*
*I'd been running away.*

## 2. Fall Season

*Fall is my favorite season*
*As a hopeless romantic*
*I want to fall in love*
*Only to fall apart*
*Before they get too close.*

*Fall is my favorite season.*
*As the leaves shed and fall*
*So do my tears*
*And suddenly I don't feel so lonely*
*As I walk on crowded streets anymore.*

*Fall is my favorite season*
*But it doesn't compare to winters*
*When the leaves are off*
*And the trees are bare*

*Covered In the cold snow*
*My soul finds peace in the silence of it all.*

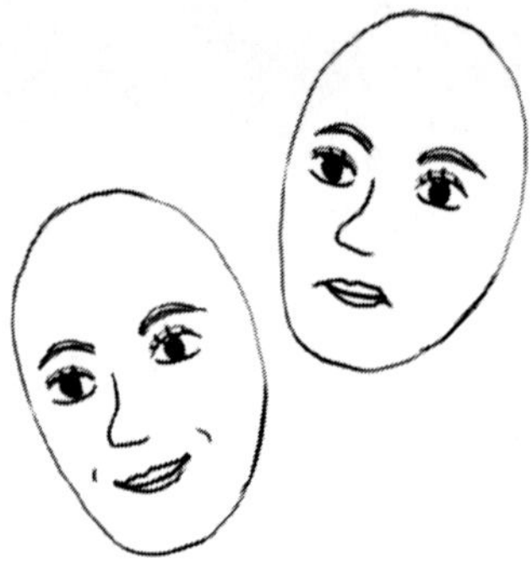

## 3. A Walking Paradox

*Who do I talk to?*
*Who do I turn to?*
*When my heart is tired,*
*And my mind hits rock bottom?*

*When I see no one around,*
*Haunting cold eyes, looking down,*
*Piercing at my reflection.*

*A sudden pause,*
*I'm numb,*
*No sorrow, no hate,*
*Nor love, nor care,*
*Just void – emotionless.*

*Is it depression or an apathetic phase?*
*'No way, no way!'*
*Too good, too young,*
*To enter that stage!*
*Throw the speculation,*
*Shut down any rage,*
*Be happy in my chaotic mess.*
*I'm a walking paradox,*
*But that's not my fault,*
*Society taught me well.*
*Let me just wear my crocs,*
*Mascara my way,*
*Fake smile on, headstrong,*
*Back to vicarious galore.*

*Sweet pretentious family talks,*
*Oozing joy at the forefront.*
*I am the perfect little girl,*
*Too sweet to ever be hurt.*

*With friends, it's another ballgame,*
*Drinking our pain away*
*Occasionally spilling banter*
*With the one that got away.*

*True friends don't judge,*
*Yet lasting bonds can get lost,*
*Underneath the veil,*
*Once you unmask.*

*Uncovered,*
*Only to reveal,*

*Sweet massacre,*
*Of childhood dreams, ambitions,*
*Once fought for, valiantly lost,*
*Long lost puppy love,*
*Now, I trust no one.*

*Realizing Life only gets hard,*
*As it comes,*
*And ships don't really last,*
*Like Titanic's tragic lovers,*
*My heart already sank.*

*Yet I carry on,*
*Hopeless romantic,*
*As I am.*

*I'm a walking paradox,*
*But that's not my fault,*
*Society taught me well.*
*Let me just wear my crocs,*
*Mascara my way,*
*Fake smile on, headstrong.*
*Back to vicarious galore.*

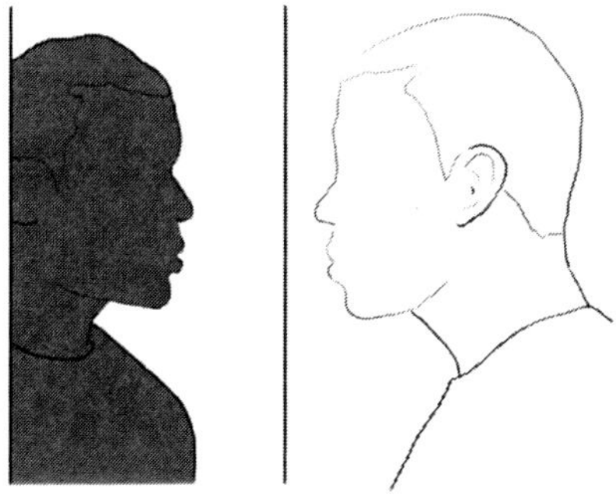

## 4. Why Do You Pretend?

*Why don't you understand?*
*What you do can impact other people*

*Why don't you understand?*
*What you say can leave it's mark on others*

*Why don't you understand?*
*All of your actions, come with consequences*
*That only you must serve.*

*The truth is,*
*I think you do understand.*
*But you pretend to ignore,*
*How deep your negligence*
*How lonely your indifference,*
*Really have kept its hold.*

*Why do you pretend*
*To be unbothered,*
*By the remarks of*
*Of those that matter?*

*Why do you pretend*
*To not care*
*About those that care about you?*

*Why do you pretend,*
*When you wake up in the morning*
*And look at the mirror*
*Why do you pretend,*
*To force a smile back when*
*You can never even face yourself?*

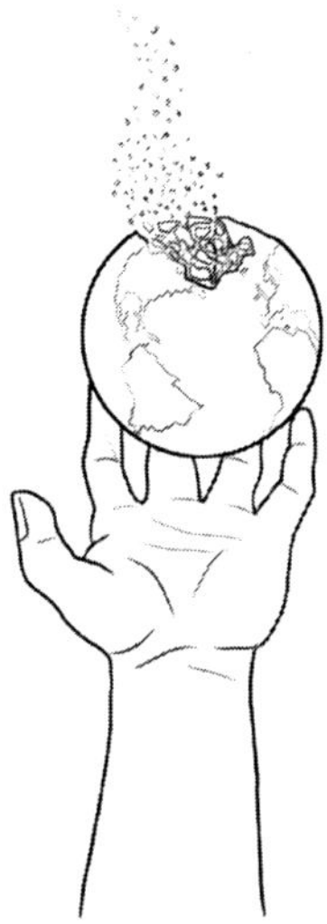

# 5. Our Illusory Reality

*We live in a world which we think is ordinary,*
*But yet is far from depicted reality,*
*Too far for us to foresee.*
*Still we suffice in the hopes of joy,*
*Despite knowing that this world is illusionary,*
*Permanently temporary,*
*Pretending to understand,*
*Yet refusing to summon why?*
*Just like we merely exist,*
*In the false assumption of living immortalized,*
*Until we're deceased.*
*Held by a fierce belief of being recreated,*
*Evolved again by this universe,*
*Just like newly sown seeds cultivated.*
*Knowing all, never realizing at all,*
*Understanding all, never visualizing at all.*

*All we are, nothing but human beings,*
*Superior breed of a living species,*
*So we think we can defy*
*Our universal functionality?*
*Thinking the end of our means lead to*
*Individual extinctions of our generations.*
*Unknown is the source how we began,*
*How we shall end,*
*Then, how can we be certain about what's in between?*

# 6. The Phase of Genius

*We are young, we are free,*
*Fiery and fierce in our competency,*
*Down for all the cheap thrills,*
*Ready for the next big nuances,*
*Invincible geniuses in our heads.*

*We are young enough;*
*Independent in our decisions to do anything we please,*
*With no fear of consequence.*

*Yet we are old enough;*
*Maturity and responsibilities seem to hit and hammer*
*along every step of the way,*
*Now more than ever.*

*We are filled with pride,*
*We have enough,*
*But never really satisfied;*
*Still on our path to self discovery,*
*Trying to achieve,*
*More than what our hearts desires.*

*As we wander with our purpose,*
*Welled up with emotions,*
*We search for an outlet,*
*Found in other wanderers just like us.*

*Building homes in one another,*
*To feel safe as we question*
*Yet quest towards*
*Our unflinching wanderlust.*

*Nevertheless, fight for our Honor,*
*We will, with armoire and stead of steel,*
*Even on the battleground,*
*Against the homes,*
*That we may have so lovingly built.*

*We are young, we are free,*
*Fiery and fierce in our competency,*
*Down for all the cheap thrills,*
*Ready for the next big nuances,*
*Invincible, geniuses in our heads.*

## 7. The City Lights

*Lighting up through the seams,*
*Bright as it can be,*
*I look out my window to see,*
*The glittering city lights in front of me.*

*City life starts as the sun dawns,*
*As day turn to night,*
*That's when the lights shine on,*
*And the city comes alive,*
*As we dream amidst the crowd.*

*One more drink,*
*One more midnight stroll,*
*One more meal,*
*Amongst the skyscrapers that are too tall,*
*Seemingly far yet all too near.*

*Carrying dreams and ambitions,*
*As these city lights light up our lives,*
*With company that numbs the pain,*
*Enough to fuel our after hours.*
*But in this concrete jungle,*
*City lights can become too blinding.*
*Amidst the massive rubble,*
*It can burn us in hindsight.*
*Beware of the lurking danger!*

*What lies ahead is not so dire…*
*As the seasons change,*
*It's bound to rain again.*
*Washing away the fire,*
*Clearing the storm,*
*Leaving behind yet another rainbow.*

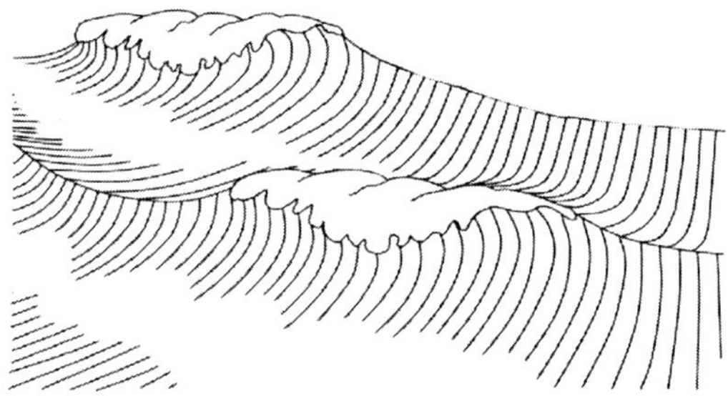

# 8. The Deep Red Ocean

*There exists a deep red ocean within all of us, which we are unaware of,*
*but with time we become proficient*
*in ripping the tides that flow against us,*
*and swimming into the depths of this ocean.*
*Although it absolutely scares us,*
*eventually we learn how to put the haunting fears behind us;*
*being left with the most humbling and gratifying feeling,*
*that is stronger than life itself,*
*the feeling of pure love and bliss.*

*All my life, I have craved*
*For a love so deep*
*That the ocean would be jealous.*
*I still don't know*

*How deep will I have to dive in,*
*To find this true love.*
*But I know I may never come close to it,*
*Unless I swim through the shallows.*
*I will never feel truly worthy,*
*Of a deep love that lifts my soul,*
*Unless i am ready to dive deep within.*
*Although, diving deep may seem scary, especially when you don't know,*
*Just how deep you need to go;*
*It can be exciting and beautiful too,*
*Once you have the will and hope.*
*The hope that one day soon,*
*Your time will come,*
*Where you'll dive the perfect dive*
*Entering the depths of the ocean of love*
*Crashing headstrong into the purest love.*
*Because hope is the closest word to home.*
*But before you go too deep,*
*To find a home in someone else.*
*Make sure you create a home,*
*Filled with hope and true love*
*Just as deep and just as true*
*For your own self.*
*No matter how hard it gets,*
*Be hopeful and headstrong.*
*What's just a blur on the surface now will eventually become clearer,*
*Through the depths of oceans within you,*
*As you find true love within yourself first.*

# 9. The Boiling Kettle

*What has life become?*
*If not a boiling kettle of tea.*

*What have we done?*
*What have we become?*
*Why are we reaping such consequences?*
*Have we done this to ourselves?*
*Have we brought this upon ourselves, really?*

*If we are to blame for all the mess*
*Then, quite frankly,*
*Maybe, we deserve this life,*
*We deserve this boiling kettle,*
*That we leave on for a little bit longer,*
*Because it's probably not boiled enough, although deep down we know it is.*

*Yet we let it boil for that extra second,*
*Until the tea reaches breaking point,*
*And finally spills right over.*
*"Ooops!.... Oh well",*
*Now the tea is useless,*
*Spilt all over the kitchen counter,*
*And needs to be thrown away.*

*Had we been a bit more mindful,*
*We could've savoured the essence,*
*The flavors, the aroma,*
*That cup of tea would've offered.*
*Now we sit in silence,*
*And deep regret.*
*Ad we realize the effort,*
*That went in boiling the tea.*
*But sadly, now we can't even enjoy it.*

*Only if we hadn't let the kettle boil*
*Just a little bit longer,*
*Only if we had known,*
*The consequences of our actions;*

*Now, who is to blame for this overpouring mess?*
*Obviously, not ourselves!*
*It's the kettle's fault, of course!*
*For going overboard.*
*How dumb can it be?*
*Does it not know when to stop?*
*When to not overdo it?*
*It literally had one job!*

*How can it be so irresponsible?*
*And mess it up?*
*What a fool!*

*So now since it is the kettle's fault*
*And nothing can be undone…*
*Once again,*
*Let's ask ourselves,*
*What have we done?*
*What have we become?*

# 10. Conflicting Emotions

*Yesterday is history,*
*Tomorrow is a mystery*
*Today is what matters*
*So can we please make the most*
*Of what we've gotten?*

*Just let the past*
*Remain in the past*
*Let's focus on things*
*That are going to make us last.*

*You don't have to sacrifice*
*Your happiness.*
*You don't have to hide away*
*From your pain*
*If you could see past this moment*

*Maybe you'd find peace in your suffering.*

*And hope to live a better future ahead*
*Lay your weary heart, and tread lighter*
*I'll help you get out of this rut*
*I promise I'll be the one that you can trust.*
*Please don't hate me,*
*On this journey*
*Because it could get ugly*
*Before it gets beautiful.*

*If you love me.*
*Let yourself bloom again*
*Because you're beautiful.*

## 11. Toxic Traits

*My toxic trait*
*Is that I tend to*
*Offer others oceans and waves*
*When all they ever deserved*
*Was a single drop of rain.*

*My toxic trait*
*Is that I crave*
*To care, to love, to nurture*
*All forms of life*
*While forgetting*
*To do the same*
*For my own self.*

*My toxic trait*
*Is that I yearn*
*To find love,*
*Safe haven*
*Happy home*
*While abandoning my own.*

## 12. Sky

*She wants to touch the sky*
*But can't see beyond the trees.*
*Who's going to tell her*
*About the stars*
*That shine beyond the seams?*

*Way above the cloudy skies*
*Her dreams go beyond this world*
*Yet she aims to touch only the sky*
*To fly as high as the next closest bird.*

*In this infinite universe*
*Where you can dream of a brand-new world*
*And infinite possibilities*
*Why is your Vision so limited*
*Your imagination so restrained*

*And your self-image so restricted?*

*When you were born*
*To not only run,*
*Nor just fly,*
*But climb, jump, swim and traverse*
*The deepest seas*
*The highest mountains*
*The brightest stars*
*That light the way*
*Across the universe and*
*Beyond these worldly realms.*

## 13. Stars in her eyes

*Glittering eyes,*
*Shining too bright,*
*For this night sky,*
*And men in sight to fathom.*

*A feminine smile,*
*A wine in hand,*
*They say there are just two things*
*That bring a lady to a tavern.*
*Love or sorrow,*
*Or maybe it's just a sense of hollow.*

*She said, She is celebrating,*
*Being welcomed back home,*
*After years of being on her own.*
*Either that or another glass of wine,*

*But who's counting when tasting stars so fine?*

# 14. Sunset Sand

*She is like the sunset*
*During the twilight hours*
*On a bright summer day.*

*She feels like a fresh breeze,*
*That blows right by the beach*
*But the more you know her,*
*The more she slips by.*

*Like the sand between your feet,*
*As you stand by the seashore.*
*While her waves crash right in,*
*Wrapping you deeper in her sandy grip*
*Hard to let her go*
*But even harder to stay,*
*Watching her slip away*

*Right under your skin.*

*Despite your efforts*
*Yet once again.*
*Maybe It's about time,*
*To let her go*
*No matter how hard it seems.*

# 15. Tiptoes

*I see you walking on your tiptoes*
*You say you're going sideways,*
*But I see you coming my way.*

*When I look at your eyes;*
*They don't shine as bright*
*As they used to before.*

*And then I see you smile,*
*But it doesn't light up your eyes,*
*No, it's not the same anymore.*

*And then we talk,*
*You speak your mind,*
*But it doesn't seem real*
*Seems like you are a facade in the face,*

*The beauty that you hold,*
*Now seems so fake.*

*Like you just don't care,*
*Like you're not there,*
*Anymore.*
*But I'll be there for you,*
*Cause I can see right through you,*
*Even if you can't see that yet.*
*I see you walking on your tip toes*
*You say you're going sideways*
*But i see you coming my way*

*I know it'll take me time*
*To find you*
*I know though you won't say it,*
*I'll wait for you.*
*And we'll find our way,*
*Back to each other,*

*I wish i could fight for you*
*Stay right beside of you.*

*No matter the distance*
*We can make it through*
*I'll do whatever it takes for you.*

*Now I'm walking on my tiptoes,*
*Though I say I'm going sideways,*
*You know I'm coming your way.*

## 16. Moth to a Flame

*It happened so fast,*
*In the glimpse of an eye,*
*I felt blinded,*
*By your emerald eyes.*

*Your piercing gaze,*
*Stripped me naked,*
*Made me feel vulnerable,*
*Than I've ever felt in my entire existence.*

*Just with one touch,*
*You made me feel truly seen,*
*And brought back the whole of my being.*

*Everyday felt like a new sunrise*
*With you by my side.*
*Uncovering each other,*
*Layer by layer,*
*I finally felt free and rediscovered.*

*Meeting You,*
*Turned my world upside down,*
*It felt more real, raw and pure,*
*Than anything I've ever felt before.*

*You made me breakdown,*
*You made me break free,*
*From my own shackles,*
*That were limiting me.*

*Not a single night,*
*Went by*
*Without me thinking*
*It's too good to be true.*

*Was this true love?*
*Or a figment of my imagination?*

*How was it possible,*
*That your embrace,*
*And your kisses,*
*Made me fall so quickly,*
*Made me heal so deeply?*

*How was it possible,*
*That I didn't even realise*
*How your love,*
*Brought me back to life?*

*I'm sorry that I had to step away,*
*Your light burned too intensely.*

*Like a moth to a flame,*
*I would've lost myself...once again.*

*Just as quickly as I'd before,*
*And you know I can't afford to do that anymore.*

*I wonder if you miss me,*
*As much as I miss you.*
*I wonder if you found the same home,*
*In me, that I found in you.*

*And if you did,*
*I wonder,*
*If falling apart hurt you,*
*Just as badly as it hurt me.*

*I wonder,*
*In the aftermath of it all,*
*What exactly was our story?*

*I wonder,*
*Were we each other's blessings?*
*Or just another one of life's lessons and learnings.*

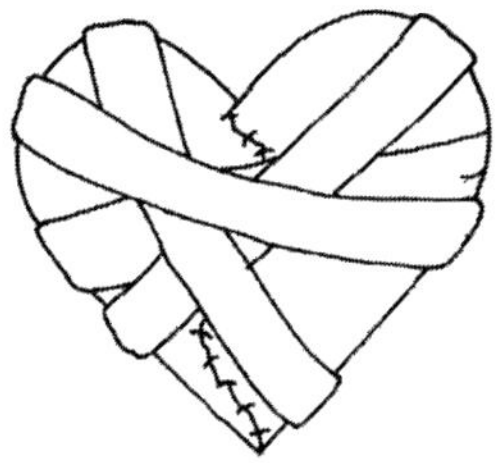

## 17. Delusional love

*It's hard to love*
*When you can't see*
*The reality for what it is.*

*But fantasize about*
*Burning romance*
*Passionate affairs*
*And reckless getaways*
*That leave you distraught.*

*It feels like my fairytale is over*
*I really wanted my story to begin*
*With 'Once Upon A Time'*
*Because you were my Prince Charming*
*And I fell deep like Cinderella.*

*I should've known better.*
*I'll admit*
*I should've thought before I let you in.*
*But this love is your illusion.*

*Take me to a place*
*With real life love,*
*I need a break*
*From this broken down fantasy.*

*Show me a place I can realize love,*
*Not just your illusions.*

## 18. A Tired Soul

*Let go of me,*
*I'm better on my own*
*This isn't me,*
*This isn't me anymore.*

*Let me be free,*
*Cause this doesn't feel like me.*

*I didn't mean to,*
*So accidentally,*
*Fall in love with you.*

*I can't afford lose myself again,*
*In the fantasy of another fairytale.*
*When I'm not looking for a shelter,*
*I am searching for a home.*

*Not a temporary relief anymore,*
*My soul is too tired to bear the ache any longer.*

*You didn't see me*
*You didn't feel my pain*
*You left me here*
*All by myself again.*

*Did you ever love me*
*Or was I just a game to you?*

*I never meant to.*
*So accidentally,*
*Fall in love with you.*

*I lost my self before,*
*Sold my soul to love.*

*Now my soul is tired*
*Of running in circles again.*

*Dear God,*
*I have worked too hard on myself*
*To bear this mess again.*

*Please let me know,*
*Will I ever really find a love,*
*That can mend,*
*My tired and yearning soul?*

# PART II
## FLIGHT: The Crash

*I may have faltered*
*But I'm still here.*

*Surviving and existing*
*Still breathing*
*Each day*
*As I recoup, and recover*
*I keep praying*
*For solace, strength and grace.*

*Wounds take time to heal*
*But exactly how long?*
*No one really knew.*

*So I decided,*
*Though I was sad and scared,*
*I'll surrender to the process.*

*Build my faith*
*In God and His plan*
*To truly restore*
*My faith within myself*
*Crying and fighting*
*To finally find a way,*
*To fly again*
*From my own cage.*

*Be undefined by my limits,*
*Rediscover my self-worth,*
*To be greater than my fears.*

## 19. Dora

*Dora*
*Always swimming in the same stream*
*Dora*
*Finding love in all the wrong scenes*
*Dora*
*Always walking down, the wrong streets*
*Dora*
*Starting whirlwinds out of dead weeds.*
*Dora*
*Let me show you how to love yourself*
*Trust me. I won't let you abandon yourself*
*Why are you always running away*
*When you have me right here?*
*Oh darling.*
*I would love you, if you let me.*

*Dora*
*Always singing to the same strings*
*Broken verses stuck on repeat.*
*Dora,*
*Don't you know that you're amazing?*
*Your Broken heart doesn't need to keep on breaking.*
*And I wish I could bring the light out of the sun*
*To help you see*
*Just how much you mean to me.*

*Oh darling,*
*Please trust me.*
*I won't ever give your heart away.*
*I'd guide you to your ocean*
*Where you truly belong,*
*Because you're so damn worthy.*

*Why are you running away?*
*When you got yourself right here.*
*Oh, I'd love you if you let me.*

## 20. Meeting My Mirror

*Knew you since we were kids,*
*But never really got to know you,*
*Until we met again as misfits.*

*Seeing your face after ages,*
*Your beauty seemed just as flawless.*
*We spoke endlessly for hours,*
*Didn't even know how the time passed,*
*And suddenly seeing you smile,*
*I felt like I'd known you my entire life.*

*It was like you reflected parts of myself,*
*That I'd always tried to hide so well,*
*From the patriarchy we live in.*

*And just like that,*
*Meeting you made me realize,*
*What I'd tried to suppress all my life.*

*Wish I could thank you*
*For helping me surrender*
*And accept my shadow self*
*That I'd always pushed away*
*Because I'm growing tired of*
*Pretending to put on a happy face.*

*Wish we could meet again*
*This time as our whole selves.*

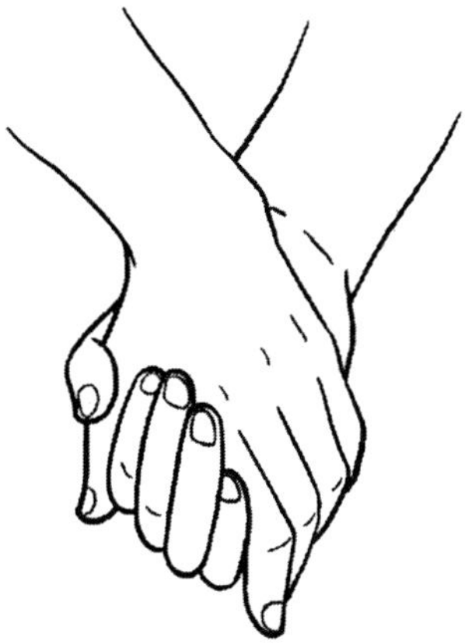

# 21. Connections

*Some people come into your lives*
*As pages, chapters and books.*

*You meet some people*
*For a reason*
*Or for a season.*

*They come to teach you lessons*
*About your life*
*And help you realize*
*Hard truths*
*That you need to accept*
*To evolve*
*Into the next chapter of your life.*

*Some people we meet,*
*Are part of our lives since forever,*
*But they are now on different pages*
*As you both outgrow and*
*Shift into different chapters of life.*

*And that's okay,*
*Because you will always find*
*New people*
*Who'll fill new pages of*
*Your life's dynamic phases.*

*And if you're lucky*
*You'll find those rare persons*
*Who you meet*
*And they instantly feel like home*
*As if you've known them*
*In another lifetime.*

*Connection that runs so deep*
*It's beyond just feelings of the heart*
*They find a way deeper within your soul.*

*Where time, place and everything else,*
*Stands still and you transcend beyond.*
*Where your silence speaks louder,*
*And you just understand*
*Everything about them*
*Without saying a single word.*

*It's like exchanging a part of you for theirs*
*And carrying it with you wherever you go.*

*You can only hope to meet them again.*
*And if you're really lucky*
*They'd stick right by your side*
*Even in this lifetime.*

# 22. You are my Poetry

*You are my poetry*
*I want to savor every inch of your skin*
*Reading every freckle and crevice*
*That's hidden beneath the surface.*

*You are my poetry*
*Intertwining perfectly in my fingertips*
*With each touch*
*With each kiss*
*I crave for more*
*As you bring me back to life.*

*You are my poetry*
*As your starry gaze*
*Catches mine*
*You light up every fiber of my being.*

*You are my poetry*
*I want to whisper words of worship*
*Lighten your burdens away.*

*I just wish to be with you,*
*Even if we fall apart someday.*

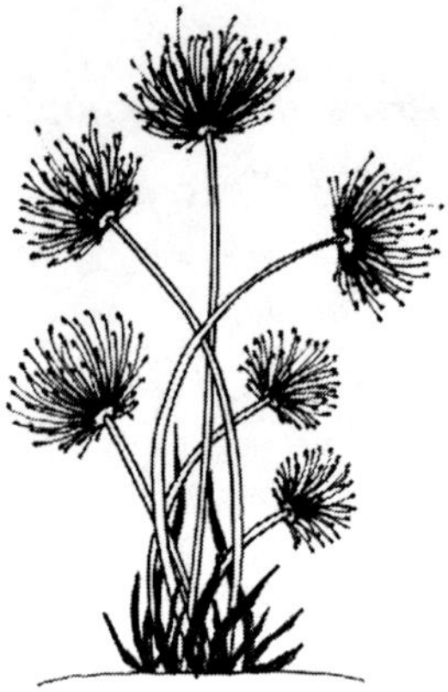

## 23. Dandelion

*There will always be*
*A little dandelion*
*That belongs to you*
*Inside of me –*

*There will always be*
*A part of you*
*That helped me*
*Find my way back*
*To love again.*

*There will always be*
*A part of you*
*That felt like home*
*That helped me grow*
*And realize all*

*My lost dream, passions and goals.*

*There will always be*
*A little dandelion*
*That belongs to you*
*That helped me heal.*

## 24. If I Sing You A Song

*If I sing you a song,*
*It's not just for the melody,*
*It's waves of emotions,*
*That arise from the depth of my soul.*

*If I sing you a song,*
*Pay attention to the lyrics*
*Hidden beneath every note.*

*They are all you need,*
*To know the feelings I can't describe.*

*If I sing you a song,*
*Notice the rhythm of my heartbeat,*
*With every tone and breath,*
*You'll find all my fears, joy, dreams,*

*And my love,*
*Flooding at its seams.*

## 25. Love Letter to my Spirit

*If you see my younger self,*
*Thank her for me.*
*She had some big dreams,*
*Aims and aspirations*
*She held on so fiercely*
*No matter what the world threw her way,*
*Despite how much the people around her*
*Laughed at her for her bizarre ways*
*She never stopped believing in herself*
*And chasing her goals.*

*Somedays more broken, scared and silent*
*Than others,*
*Yet she never gave up on herself*
*She kept going,*
*And she still keeps going.*

*She is resilient and rough like that*
*But there's a softness in her strength,*
*And a quietness in her confidence,*
*That comes from within.*

*She turned her pain into power*
*By loving herself,*
*Fiercely, unapologetically and truly.*

*She built a better me today*
*Through all her misguided pieces.*

*She is a fighter*
*She is a warrior*
*She is true to her core.*
*She is rising all over again.*
*And for that I am eternally grateful,*
*To my young relentless spirit.*

## 26. Where Is Home?

*I ride, into the horizon where the sun and moon collide,*
*I lie, by the bay surrounding the endless sea,*
*I reside where the sun dawns and the waves come crashing down to a standstill*
*Welcome to my home, where the sun, sand and moon finally meet.*

*"But which place do you reside in?"*
*People ask out of curious intent.*
*I say,*
*My home is not a place, it is rather a state.*
*A state of joy, hope, love and light.*

*A state of wholesomeness in the fragmented mess*
*Of living truly,*
*Even if things get unruly.*

*Where I can be unapologetically me,*
*Completely free,*
*Uncaged by fears and doubts of my own being.*

*Where I can run and reign unabashedly,*
*Cry or laugh unequivocally.*
*This state of being,*
*That is Home for me.*

*That is the place where I reside in.*

*So as the dusk turns to dawn,*
*Now you know where I will be…*
*I ride, into the horizon where the sun and moon collide,*
*I lie, by the bay surrounding the endless sea,*
*I reside where the sun dawns and the waves come crashing down to a standstill,*
*Welcome to my home, where the sun, sand and moon finally meet.*

## 27. Can we take a minute?

*Can we take a minute?*
*To appreciate the beauty of our universe*
*That we are blessed to live in?*

*Or is it so hard to see it*
*With our everyday responsibilities*
*Are we incapable of feeling serene*
*Any more than we are incapable of*
*Working towards anything*
*Beyond the sense of security and monetary benefits?*

*Why are you trying so hard to run*
*While you are constantly racing inside*
*The hamsters wheel.*

*What lies beyond;*
*Have you ever tried to unleash?*
*What even is normal?*
*When you don't even know your true potential*
*How will you find your purpose*
*If you are so scared to even find*
*Your true self beneath the surface.*

*Can we take a minute?*
*To understand ourselves truly*
*To appreciate beyond what we can see.*

*Can we take a minute?*
*To appreciate the beauty of our universe*
*That we are blessed to live in.*

# 28. Creating my Home

*Trying to find my way back home.*
*Oh darling, don't you worry about me,*
*I'll be okay on my own.*

*All my life, I've been running away*
*Trying to escape*
*From familiar faces,*
*And crowded places.*

*Just to find myself again*
*When I was just a little girl,*
*I travelled the world around*
*Made memories so profound,*
*Felt like I finally belonged,*
*Until I left to fly again.*

*Working a few odd jobs,*
*Struggling to stay afloat,*
*Switching careers like clothes,*
*Still struggling to pay rent*
*For a strangers home.*
*I got lost in familiar faces*
*I've roamed in famous places,*
*Always surrounded by people*
*Yet could never really be my true self.*

*Trying to find my way back home;*
*Oh darling, don't you worry about me*
*I'll be okay on my own.*

*Swimming against the waves,*
*Running against the hurdle ahead,*
*Tried to carry the extra weight*
*Of mountains and regrets.*

*I was searching for myself*
*Everywhere else*
*But within my own self.*

*That's where I realized*
*Lies my joy, peace and happiness.*

*I am coming back to my home,*
*Making myself my safe space now*
*Oh darling I am whole now.*
*On my own.*

# 29. Hurricane

*If you think it*
*You believe it*
*You create it*
*You have the power to*
*Create endless hurricanes*
*That can destroy everything in its wake.*

*But that also means*
*You have the power to create waves*
*That can save burning bridges and*
*Carry lost ships back to its shore.*

*So, tell me,*
*What are you creating with the waves of your mind?*

## 30. Dolphin Dive

*I am constantly,*
*Swimming against the waves,*
*And I'm glad about it*
*For a change.*

*For I do not drown,*
*I leap for air,*
*And swim on my way*
*Against the endless waves,*
*Riptides and hurricanes,*
*Amidst the deep blue waters.*

*These waves of worry and shame,*
*Oceans of fury and vain,*
*Have made me one hell of a swimmer.*

*As I glide through it all,*
*With a steady gaze, straight ahead,*
*Shore in sight,*
*I smile and I align,*
*With each breath,*
*And leap of faith,*
*Because I know I'm in the right lane.*

*I am closer to my true happiness,*
*Like a dolphin, I come up for every breath,*
*Diving back in,*
*With effortless love and grace,*
*Swimming in my own benevolence.*

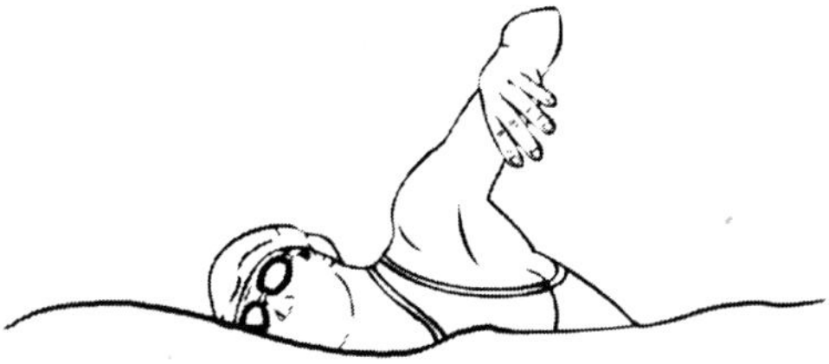

## 31. Tidal Waves

*I always thought I was a good swimmer*
*Until my own waves drowned me*
*And left my body*
*In another tide of agony.*

*But I remembered*
*That I can hold my breath*
*Even though I'm underwater*
*Even though I'm struggling*
*To resurface right now.*

*I have been trained*
*To keep swimming*
*Despite all odds.*

*I had faith*
*In my ability*
*To hold my breath a little longer.*
*To keep going a little further.*

*I had faith*
*In the waves*
*Even though they were too much to bear*
*Every storm has to come to an end someday.*

*Time and tides never stand still,*
*But after the rain, the sun will be rising,*
*And the ocean will be calm again.*

*I know I'm strong enough,*
*To resurface through this pain.*

*Even though I feel like I'm drowning,*
*There's a new beginning,*
*Awaiting after the end,*
*Of the horizon ahead.*

## 32. Gravity

*For longer than I remember,*
*Gravity kept holding me back,*
*From chasing my dreams.*

*My life seemed to backtrack*
*One step forward 20 steps back.*

*Gravity kept me stuck*
*In the middle of the night*
*With endless thoughts*
*That almost ate me alive.*

*Would I ever be free*
*From the cages of my own mind?*
*Would I ever be able to love*
*And live a life*

*I'd always aspired to lead?*
*Would I ever be able to break free*
*From my own depression and anxiety?*
*Will I ever find peace, joy and light*
*In this reality?*

*Gravity always worked against me*
*Gravity only broke me down.*
*Until one day I had enough,*
*Gravity got me to break through*
*And create my own reality.*

*Once forgotten old dreams,*
*Resurfaced back to life.*
*I was scared that the best days were behind me*
*But suddenly the haze turned to clarity.*
*Gravity turned my dreams into reality*
*And brought my soul back to the light.*

*So tomorrow,*
*Even if gravity breaks down*
*Everything I've ever build,*
*I'll be prepared.*

*For I've worked too damn hard,*
*For it to ever break my spirit.*

*The fire in me will keep burning,*
*Now that I know my worth,*
*Is too damn powerful.*
*I know I can defy gravity's game itself.*

# PART III

## FLIGHT: The Rise Again

*What a year it's been,*
*And I'm still healing.*
*This time, not out of fear,*
*But out of self-love.*

*I can feel the wounds closing in*
*As my wings are being restored*
*And the wind is finally flowing*
*In a direction that serves me better.*

*Just a matter of time*
*Before I get back up*
*And take flight.*

*This time*
*Not to find myself*
*Nor to lose myself*
*In new worlds and realities.*

*But to create*
*My own happiness*
*To chase my dreams*
*Passions and my purpose*
*As I recreate experiences*
*While really living for myself.*

*For now, I am found within myself.*
*For now, I am my own home and solace.*
*For now, I've learnt to say NO*
*To anything that's draining my energy,*
*Because NO WAY, am I ever losing sight*
*Of my own self ever again.*

## 33. Morning Light

*Out the door*
*Lies a world, lies a life, lies a soul*
*As we phase into the morning light*
*Into clear blue skies, we'll be safe and sound*
*We'll be alright*
*Alter times*
*Alter seasons*
*Alter minds*
*Alter situations*
*As dusk turn to dawn*
*We'll be fighting through it all*
*Pain turned into power*
*Fear turned into freedom*
*Crisis turned into calm*
*Darkness turned into light*
*Out the door*

*Lies our freedom, lies our soul*
*As tonight turns into the morning light*
*As the moon creeps into the night*
*And the stars shine in our hindsight*
*Let's dream of a new morning light.*

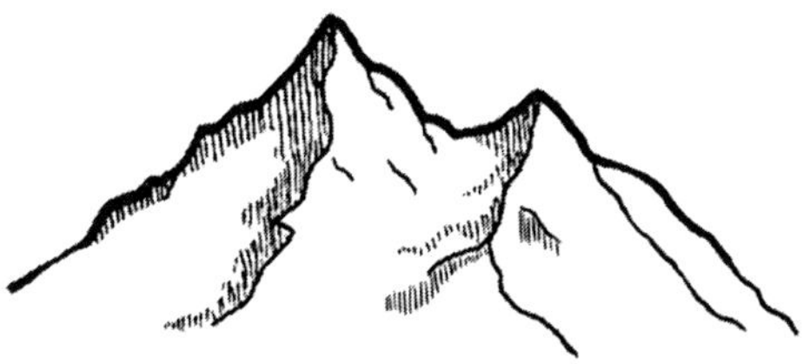

## 34. Strength

*True strength*
*Lies not in numbers*
*But in your solitude.*
*It's in your experiences*
*And the struggles*
*That you faced.*

*True strength*
*Is not just about physical health*
*Nor is it about material wealth*
*It's in knowing your inner self*
*And stepping into your light embrace.*

*True strength*
*Is not confidence*
*Nor competence*

*It's earned with everything*
*You unlearn to live again.*

*True strength*
*Is true love, honor, care and respect*
*For your internal self.*
*Once you find*
*Your true inner strength*
*It's bound to reflect*
*Unshakeable resilience and grit*
*In your outer world*
*With effortless ease and grace.*

## 35. Reconstruct your Beauty

*Don't let socially constructed ideas about beauty lower your self-esteem.*
*There are no rules to beauty.*
*Accept and love yourself as you truly are.*
*Embrace your flaws and get comfortable in your own skin.*

*Wear your imperfections like they don't need a season to be fashionable.*
*Feel all your feelings, release your pent-up emotions and and own your truth.*
*Only you can truly heal and let go of all the restrictions that are tying you down.*

*Stop playing small for others comfort.*
*Be strong, resilient and truly believe in yourself and your self worth.*
*Even if that means making people uncomfortable with your personal growth.*
*Let go of patterns that no longer serve you.*

*You were meant to play BIG and follow your heart to your true calling.*
*You're just getting started. Don't stop now.*
*Darling. This is just the first page of your fresh new story!*
*The rest is yet to be written.*

*So hold out your pens. And speak your truth. And don't give a damn about others being knocked off their high horse.*
*You know you deserve better anyway.*
*So, find that trust in you and see how you draw people, places and things meant for you closer with each passing day.*

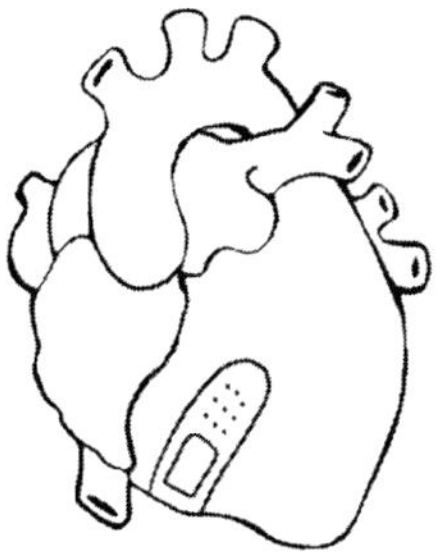

# 36. As I Am Healing

*As I'm healing-*
*I am learning*
*That only I can set myself free.*

*As I'm healing-*
*I am learning*
*To love every piece of me.*

*As I'm healing-*
*I am handling*
*My sharp edges and swords more gracefully.*

*As I'm healing-*
*I am realizing*
*The infinite potential and resilience I carry.*

*As I'm healing-*
*I am choosing*
*My peace, joy and love above all else.*

*As I'm healing-*
*I'm crying, laughing, falling and rising.*
*From the ashes of my shadows*
*That have turned to light.*

*As I'm healing-*
*I am escaping the cages that no longer serve me,*
*I am spreading my wings as I take flight.*

## 37. Commitment to Myself

*As I commit to my self-love journey,*
*I practice what I preach*
*With self-awareness,*
*Full of grace and compassion.*

*With each day that passed*
*I patiently wait to unload*
*The years of tension & burdens I carry*
*Knowing the more I let go*
*The more my wounds would heal.*

*Opening up to the light within,*
*Feeling love and happiness*
*That shines from nowhere else*
*But the source in me.*

*I promise to share all my lessons*
*To speak my truth*
*And embrace my journey*
*With all those I meet along the way.*

## 38. Resilience

*Every failure,*
*Every challenge,*
*Every setback,*
*Has build my Resilience.*

*Whenever I was overwhelmed*
*There was a voice that said*
*Focus on the next step*
*Not the entire staircase.*
*Slowly but surely*
*I kept climbing ahead.*

*I have always been wise*
*But too afraid to face the circumstances.*
*But now I've been gaining strength,*
*To face the hurdles lying ahead.*

*Now that I've gone through,*
*My darkest and weakest moments*
*I have faced, lived and set myself free*
*From all the fear that used to take over me.*

*I've crossed the hurdles*
*I've overcome the challenges*
*And I've embraced the setbacks*
*That lived rent free in my mind,*
*And replayed by life at every turn.*

*I know now,*
*That I'm almost at the end of my dark tunnel*
*Close enough to see the light*
*Of the world outside.*

*As I re-emerge,*
*I'll look back at my darkest days,*
*And feel nothing but deep gratitude,*
*For never giving up,*
*On the person I know I was always meant to be.*

## 39. Life's Tests

*Life tests us in many*
*Different, difficult, and weird ways.*

*We can only hope to grow wise,*
*With the little signs of learnings,*
*And better ourselves as we rise,*
*Through Life's lessons and teachings.*

*As we learn, we grow,*
*Or so we are told.*

*Stay in the present, feel your presence,*
*It's the solution to all your woes and worries,*
*For you can only suffer,*
*In your imagination or your memory,*
*Or so we are told.*

*Since yesterday is history,*
*Tomorrow is a mystery,*
*Today is what truly matters.*
*Yet why does it get harder to face reality?*

*As we hope for better days,*
*Because of the impending uncertainty,*
*I fear it's not too late,*
*Yet to seek happier times ahead,*
*Until our longevity.*

*In this world, we are born to dwell in,*
*There is a lot to see and yet to accomplish,*
*All my dreams, hopes and goals,*
*Seem either too close,*
*Or too good to be true.*
*But the choice lies with me,*
*Whether to pursue,*
*Or just let them fade within.*

*With so many thoughts brewing inside,*
*I can't help but feel stuck,*
*Time and time again in my mind,*
*Between pursuing my passions,*
*Wishing upon luck,*
*Yet feeling too drained,*
*Amidst counting down the days,*
*Wherever I may traverse.*

*As I pray to God, I ask,*
*Can this weight ever lift off my chest?*
*Although we arrive with baggage we detest,*
*I felt weak to carry on these burdens;*
*So I am trying to get stronger,*
*To do justice to my shoulders,*
*As I can't foresee for how long,*
*This weight shall stay on,*
*But as long as it does,*
*At least it won't feel as heavy.*

*Because I finally believe in my ability,*
*To lift myself up despite my insecurities,*
*And stride along,*
*Feeling grateful and ready,*
*To just let it go and belong in this reality.*

## 40. Karma

*The best revenge*
*Is no revenge at all*
*But being so focused on your growth*
*That you are unbothered*
*By their actions.*

*The best revenge*
*Is to stand up for your self*
*Give yourself the respect you deserve*
*And reclaim your own power.*

*The best revenge*
*Is letting those who don't know*
*Talk all that they want*
*While you step away*
*And let Karma take care of the rest.*

*The best revenge*
*Is in owning your truth*
*And finally using your inner voice*
*Don't just silence yourself*
*To make them comfortable.*

*You were born to be true*
*To be authentically you*
*Protect yourself fiercely.*
*Don't let others define you*
*Influence you,*
*Belittle you,*
*Walk all over you.*

*Don't dim your light for others sake.*
*Let your soul shine bright.*
*Let it inspire, instigate or ignite others,*
*It's not your job to heal them anyway,*
*That's their karma to bear.*

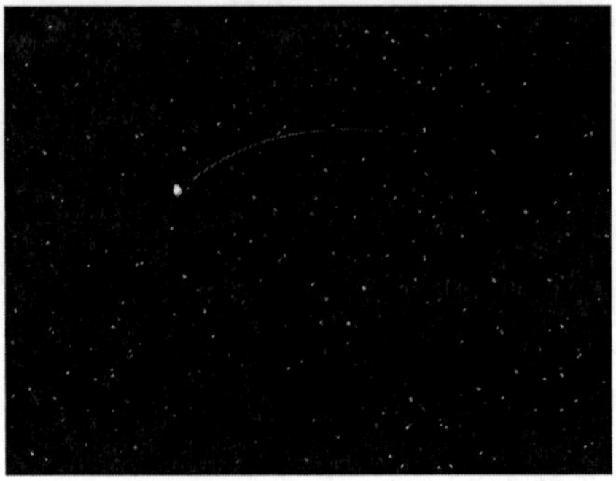

## 41. Destiny

*Maybe we are all destined*
*For this journey*
*Of self-discovery*
*From the very beginning.*

*Like caterpillar,*
*We are born to let go*
*Of our safe spaces*
*To outgrow our comfort cocoon*
*Over and over again.*

*Until we transmute*
*Into a butterfly*
*Towards the next destination*
*And fall again*
*That's the only way*

*To go through*
*Grow through*
*Life and all it's changing times.*

*Forever evolving*
*Into the next chapter*
*By grace through faith.*

*So don't be afraid*
*To fly and*
*To fall back down*
*And rise again.*

*I pray that you believe in yourself*
*Throughout your journey*
*Even if you do hit rock bottom.*

*Keep your dreams close*
*Especially in the darkest nights.*
*For they'll lead you*
*Exactly where you're meant to go*
*In this lifetime.*

*Don't settle for a mediocre life*
*When you have so much potential*
*To re-write your own destiny.*

## 42. She is a Queen

*She's a Queen*
*That cannot be dethroned.*

*Because*

*She's a Queen*
*Of her own throne*
*Of her own world.*
*With a force*
*To be reckoned with.*
*She entered her life*
*With a pure heart of gold*
*But the world turned it to dust*
*Now she's flipped the script*
*And emerged like a diamond*
*From the same dust.*

*She's a Queen*
*Who has not only found herself*
*But rebuild her entire existence.*

*She's a Queen*
*Of her own mind*
*She can't be dethroned*
*By anyone else but God Himself.*

## 43. Step Into Your Power

*The only way*
*To step fully*
*Into your power*

*Is by letting go*
*And surrender*
*Who you think you need to be.*

## 44. Be Divine

*As I am filling my own cup,*
*Being my own muse,*
*Recognizing my own worth*
*Standing up for myself*

*Loving my own self*
*Praising my existence*
*Validating my personal growth*
*Owning my own truth*

*Admiring my own reflection*
*And living my own journey of life…*

*I realize I am one*
*With the divine source of creation.*

*I imbibe within me*
*A nurturing soul of a Goddess.*

*As I recognize my purpose*
*As I come to terms with*
*My power, my worth and my potential*
*I'm ready to re-live and re-love life again.*
*But I will tread with fierce strength*
*Balancing my softness only*
*For those who deserve it.*

*Now I extend my energy*
*Only to those who are truly worthy*
*Of receiving and basking in its glory.*

*I'm creating my own reality*
*And it's nothing short of a paradise.*

## 45. Release

*Let's release,*
*All the baggage we carry*
*All the burdensome worries*
*All the problems we marry.*

*Let's release,*
*What no longer serves us*
*Wounds that still hurt our heart*
*Bonds that make us fall apart.*

*Let's release,*
*All our past mistakes*
*All our temptations and vices*
*All our own limiting ways.*

*Let's release,*
*Our past versions of self*
*And learn to re-live*
*And reconnect with our authentic self.*

*Let's release,*
*So we can re-write our own fate*
*Reclaim our true potential*
*As we begin again.*

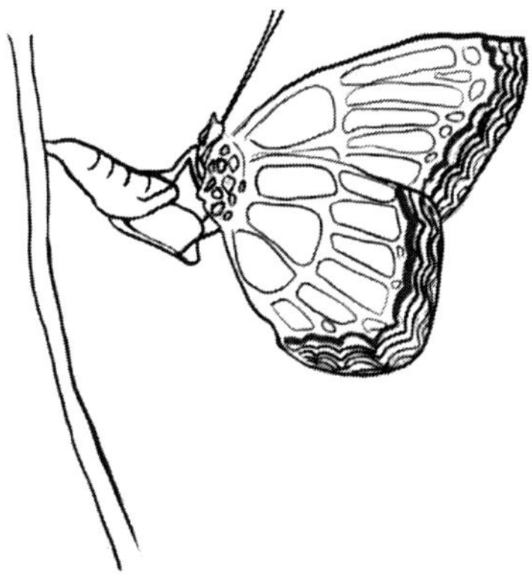

## 46. New Wings

*Today,*
*There's a new beginning,*
*Re-emerging*
*As I am resurfacing*
*From the depth of the oceans*
*That flooded my mind.*

*Today,*
*I feel revived,*
*Renewed, reborn,*
*Blessed to witness*
*A second chance at life.*

*Today,*
*As I embrace my soul*
*And restore faith in my spirit*

*My heart is growing new wings.*

*To fly higher*
*To turn dreams into reality*
*To turn my thoughts into action.*

*With every fall,*
*I rise higher.*
*With every breakthrough,*
*I finally break free.*

## 47. Rise Like A Phoenix

*Everyday,*
*You are reborn from the ashes of our past.*
*A little older, a little wiser, always hoping for a little more.*

*Just like a phoenix,*
*You are reborn, once again,*
*From the ashes of your past life.*

*Let go of all your fears,*
*Because after every fall,*
*You're meant to fly higher,*
*To live a great life of meaning and purpose.*

*So, get ready,*
*To fall and rise back up again.*

*Believe in yourself, fearlessly,*
*Fly high like a Phoenix.*

# ABOUT THE AUTHOR

If you ask Saee Joshi to define herself, she will probably say that she is a walking paradox, who finally found her release through creativity.

She was born in India, brought up in the Middle East and completed her studies in the UK. Having such a multi - culturally diverse upbringing, rightly so, she picked up a range of multi-faceted interests from a very young age.

Two of these interests stuck with her from childhood until today: Writing and Music!

As a schoolkid, she would often write random day-to-day thoughts in her secret diary! As a teen, these random thoughts started including random song lyrics and poems too. Ever since then, she has grown and expanded her creativity through marketing!

She is a passionate content writer, brand strategist and digital marketer with 5 years of experience in the field of marketing; who is currently working as a copywriter at one of the fastest growing agencies in Abu Dhabi, UAE called digitalfarm.

In her spare time, she also works as a freelance content marketer who aims to help clients build and grow strong digital brands through organic content marketing strategies. Her expertise lies in the wide spectrum of digital marketing, design, content and copywriting, where she can integrate her creative and analytical sides to create content for brands.

She also functions as a singer, songwriter, poet and a cat lover in her spare time. She has released her debut single "Pieces of Me" available on all streaming platforms.
Do check it out! (links mentioned below)

Today, as a copywriter, marketer, writer and a singer. She is officially a running paradox, with even more hats to don than ever before. But all hats and labels aside, she is a creator at heart and a true artist in her soul!

**Check out her personal blog:**

The Millennial Way to read more of her personal blog articles, pieces and poems and to stay updated on her next upcoming book! ;)

Also, check out her projects to know more about her professional skills and stay updated with her work – www.millennialaces.com

Finally, follow her social media channels for all the latest updates!

**Linkedin**: https://linkedin.com/in/saeejoshii
**Instagram**: https://instagram.com/saeejoshiiofficial
**YouTube**: SAEE J MUSIC

*For more lnfo, Just...*

SCAN ME

## Writer's Pocket

Writer's Pocket is a publication house established in 2016. We began with the aim of providing a better publishing platform for aspiring writers and budding poets.

The publishing industry in India (and around the world, to a great extent) is always something of a mystery even to the writers themselves. We are working on making publishing more accessible to everyone.

So far, we have helped over 3,000 writers turn their dreams into reality by publishing the books and continue to do so. By doing so, we also provide some of the best content by Indian writers to the readers.